Lingo Dingo
and the
French chef

Written by Mark Pallis
Illustrated by James Cottell

For my awesome sons Oscar and Felix- MP

For Leo and Juniper - JC

LINGO DINGO AND THE FRENCH CHEF

All rights reserved. This book or any portion thereof may not be reproduced or used in any manner whatsoever without the express written permission of the publisher except for the use of brief excerpts in a review.

Story edited by Natascha Biebow, Blue Elephant Storyshaping
First Printing, 2022
ISBN: 978-1-913595-53-1
NeuWestendPress.com

Lingo Dingo
and the
French chef

Written by Mark Pallis
Illustrated by James Cottell

NEU WESTEND
— PRESS —

This is Lingo. She's a Dingo and she loves helping. Anyone. Anytime. Anyhow.

Lingo often helps her stylish neighbour Gunther, who lives by himself next door. She does a few jobs and has a nice chat. It makes Gunther feel good and it makes Lingo feel good too.

One day, Lingo arranged a special birthday party for Gunther. She even ordered a cake from a famous French chef.

There was a knock at the door, "It must be the cake!" said Lingo. But it was a monkey.

"Bonjour. Je m'appelle Chef Nono. J'ai un problème," he said.

Oh no. I can't speak French yet, thought Lingo. *Maybe 'Bonjour' is like 'Hello'.*

Bonjour = Hello; **Je m'appelle** = My name is; **J'ai un problème** = I have a problem

"Bonjour," said Lingo. Chef Nono replied slowly, "Je suis désolé. Je ne peux pas faire le gâteau d'anniversaire."

"I don't understand," said Lingo. "But let me guess. You want…"

Je suis désolé = I am sorry; **Je ne peux pas faire** = I cannot make; **le gâteau d'anniversaire** = the birthday cake

"Mon four est brisé," explained Chef. "Puis-je utiliser votre four ?"

Chef's oven must be broken thought Lingo. "I know! Let's bake the cake together," she said.

Mon four est brisé = my oven is broken;
Puis-je utiliser votre four = can I use your oven?

Chef tapped his wrist. "Quelle heure est-il ? Neuf heures ? Dix heures ?" he asked.

Lingo pointed at her watch.

"Onze heures ! ? Allons-y. Vite !"
They only had one hour until the party.

Quelle heure est-il? = what time is it?; **neuf heures** = nine o'clock; **dix heures** = ten o'clock; **onze heures** = eleven o'clock; **allons-y** = let's go; **vite** = quick

Chef Nono and Lingo whizzed around the kitchen:

Un tablier pour vous.

Un fouet.

Un bol à mélanger.

un tablier pour vous = an apron for you; **un fouet** = a whisk;
un bol à mélanger = a mixing bowl

"Passez-moi le beurre, le sucre, les œufs et la farine, s'il vous plaît," said Chef.

Lingo wasn't sure what those words meant, so she just grabbed fish, coffee and onions instead.

Poisson, café et oignons. Dégoûtant !" laughed Chef.

passez-moi = pass me; **le beurre** = the butter; **le sucre** = the sugar; **les œufs** = the eggs; **et la farine** = and the flour; **s'il vous plaît** = please; **poisson** = fish; **café** = coffee; **oignons** = onions; **dégoûtant** = disgusting

Chef plopped sugar, butter, eggs and flour into a bowl. "So that's what 'sucre, beurre, œufs, farine' means!" laughed Lingo.

"Je mélange, tu mélanges, nous mélangeons," said Chef and together they began to mix the cake.

je mélange = I mix; **tu mélanges** = you mix; **nous mélangeons** = we mix

"Finallement, la levure chimique. Deux cuillerées," said Chef. Lingo guessed 'la levure chimique' meant baking powder, but how much?

Before she could ask, Chef hurried away, saying, "Excusez-moi, je dois faire pipi."

Lingo laughed, "I can guess what 'pipi' means!"

Finallement = finally; **la levure chimique** = baking powder; **deux cuillerées** = two spoonfulls; **excusez-moi** = excuse me; **je dois faire pipi** = I need to do a wee wee

I wonder if this is too much? thought Lingo as she added ten spoonfulls of 'levure chimique' to the mix.

She carefully put everything into the oven and before long, a sweet cakey smell filled the kitchen.

la levure chimique = baking powder

"Que s'est-il passé ? C'est énorme," said Chef.

Lingo realised she had added too much baking powder.
"Sorry," she said sheepishly.

que s'est-il passé = what happened; **c'est énorme** = it's huge

"I know what will make you feel better," said Lingo, kindly. "Eat this 'cornichon'!"

"Dégoûtant ! Je déteste les cornichons." said Chef.

They were running out of time.

dégoûtant = disgusting; **je déteste les cornichons** = I hate gherkins

"I've got it! Gunther loves hats, so let's turn the cakey mess into a hat cake!" said Lingo.

First she shaped the cake, then she filled balloons with icing.

Next came the best part: POP! POP! POP!

It was a messy job but in the end, the cake looked fantastic. "Rouge, orange, jaune, vert, bleu. Fantastique!" said Chef.

rouge = red; **orange** = orange; **jaune** = yellow;
vert = green; **bleu** = blue; **fantastique** = fantastic

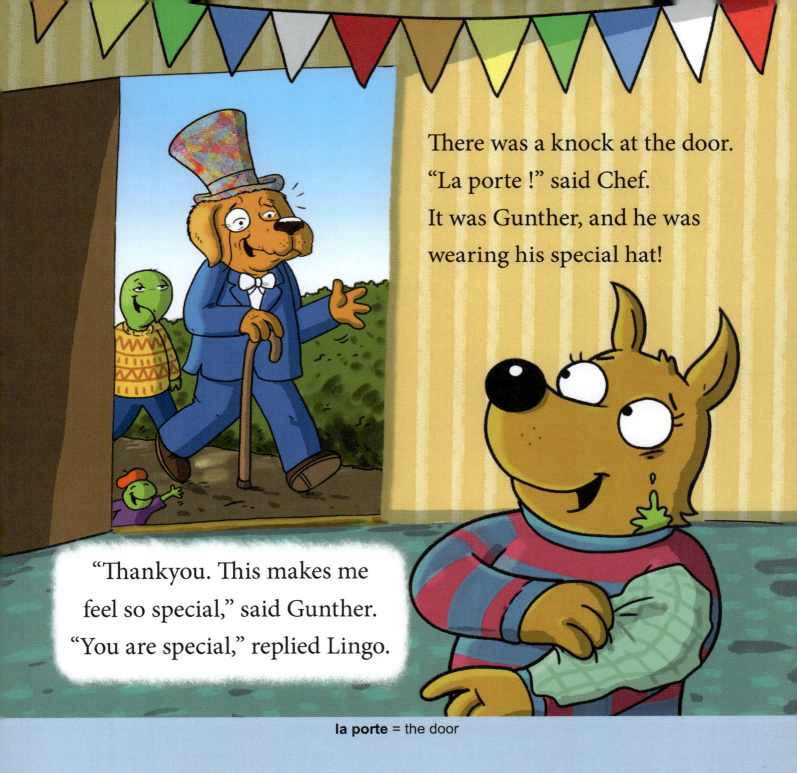

There was a knock at the door.
"La porte !" said Chef.
It was Gunther, and he was wearing his special hat!

"Thankyou. This makes me feel so special," said Gunther.
"You are special," replied Lingo.

la porte = the door

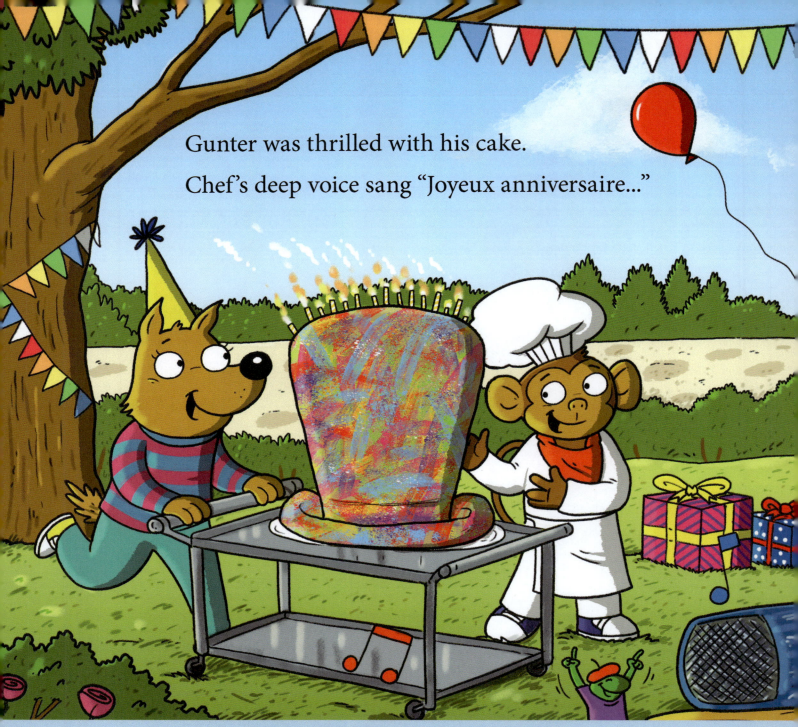

Gunter was thrilled with his cake.

Chef's deep voice sang "Joyeux anniversaire..."

joyeux anniversaire = happy birthday to you

"Soufflez!" said Chef.

Gunther blew out all the candles in one puff and everyone tucked in.

soufflez = blow

"Je mange, tu manges, il mange, elle mange, ils mangent." laughed Chef.

"Nous mangeons !" added Lingo proudly.

je mange = I eat; **tu manges** = you eat; **il mange** = he eats; **elle mange** = she eats; **ils mangent** = they eat; **we eat** = we eat

Lingo, Gunther and Chef watched the sun go down.

"Je suis heureux,
 tu es heureux,
  nous sommes heureux," said Chef.

je suis heureux = I am happy; **tu es heureux** = you are happy; **nous sommes heureux** = he is happy

Baking a cake, helping a friend, learning a new language... what a day!

But now it was time for bed. It was time to dream about all the fun things that might happen tomorrow.

Learning to love languages

An additional language opens a child's mind, broadens their horizons and enriches their emotional life. Research has shown that the time between a child's birth and their sixth or seventh birthday is a "golden period" when they are most receptive to new languages. This is because they have an in-built ability to distinguish the sounds they hear and make sense of them. The Story-powered Language Learning Method taps into these natural abilities.

How the Story-powered language learning Method works

We create an emotionally engaging and funny story for children and adults to enjoy together, just like any other picture book. Studies show that social interaction, like enjoying a book together, is critical in language learning.

Through the story, we introduce a relatable character who speaks only in the new language. This helps build empathy and a positive attitude towards people who speak different languages. These are both important aspects in laying the foundations for lasting language acquisition in a child's life.

As the story progresses, the child naturally works with the characters to discover the meanings of a wide range of fun new words. Strategic use of humour ensures that this subconscious learning is rewarded with laughter; the child feels good and the first seeds of a lifelong love of languages are sown.

For more information and free learning resources visit www.neuwestendpress.com

You can learn more words and phrases with these hilarious, heartwarming stories from NEU WESTEND PRESS

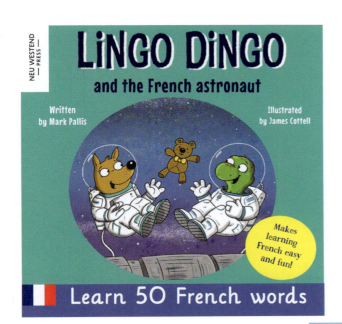
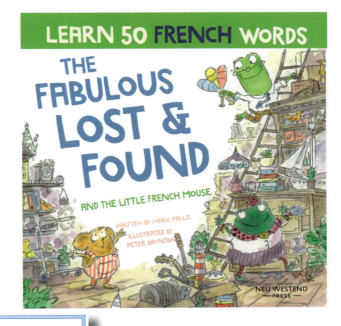

@MARK_PALLIS on twitter
www.neuwestendpress.com

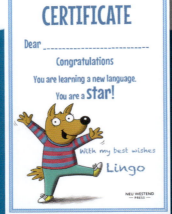

To download your FREE certifcate, and more cool stuff, visit
www.neuwestendpress.com

@jamescottell on INSTAGRAM
www.jamescottellstudios.co.uk

"I want people to be so busy laughing, they don't realise they're learning!"
Mark Pallis

Crab and Whale is the bestselling story of how a little Crab helps a big Whale. It's carefully designed to help even the most energetic children find a moment of calm and focus. It also includes a special mindful breathing exercise and affirmation for children. Also available in French as 'Crabe et Baleine.'

Featured as one of Mindful.org's 'Seven Mindful Children's books'

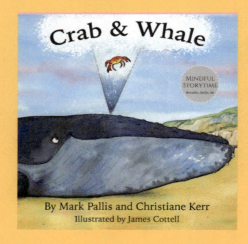

Do you call them hugs or cuddles?

In this funny, heartwarming story, you will laugh out loud as two loveable gibbons try to figure out if a hug is better than a cuddle and, in the process, learn how to get along.

A perfect story for anyone who loves a hug (or a cuddle!)

www.markpallis.com

Printed in Great Britain
by Amazon